smart interiors

Publisher: Carles Broto
Architectural Advisor: Pilar Chueca
Graphic designer & production: Oriol Vallès
Text: contributed by the architects, edited by Jacobo Krauel and
Amber Ockrassa

© Carles Broto i Comerma
Jonqueres, 10, 1-5
08003 Barcelona, Spain
Tel.: +34 93 301 21 99
 Fax: +34-93-301 00 21
E-mail: info@linksbooks.net
www. linksbooks.net

ISBN: 84-96263-25-8

Printed in China 2005

smart
interiors

INDEX

Introduction 7

Arthur Collin architect
Loft Apartment in Clerkenwell 8

5th Studio
Eden Street / Clarendon Street 14

Werner Van dermeersch
Hose Arnold-Berghmans 24

Patrick Genard & Ass.
House T 30

Marco Savorelli Architects
Apartament in Milan 40

Eligio Novello Arch EPFL
House Troesch-Tschan 48

Ottorino Bersilli & Cecilia Cassina
Ristrutturazione in Manerbio 56

Waro Kishi & K. Associates
House in Shimogamo 64

Koh Kitayama
Omni Quarter 70

Sergio Calatroni
Gallery Uchida 76

Bruce Kuwabara & Evan Webber
Residence and Studio in Richmond Hill 82

Valerio Dewalt Train
Gardner Residence
90

Koh Kitayama
Plane + House
98

Harry Seidler & Associates
Farrell House
104

Randy Brown
Study Residence in Omaha
110

Dieter Thiel
Bangert Studio and House
122

José Cruz Ovalle
Study and Home in Vitacura
128

Michael Szyszkowitz & Karla Kowalski
Home Office for a Psychotherapist
134

Dick van Gameren & Mastenbroek
Kantoor en Penthouse
138

Francesco Delogu & Gaetano Lixi
Castello Catrani
144

Julia B. Bolles & Peter L. Wilson
Dub House
150

Rataplan
Bürombau Vienna Paint
156

Arnaud Goujon AtchitecteDPLG
Transformed penthouse
162

smartinteriors

Introduction

Interior design is one of the fields of architecture that has most evolved in recent decades. Dynamic new trends and changes are seen in the creative use of materials and in unprecedented construction styles.

In response to increasingly discerning clients with a growing range of stipulations, architects working in interior design have been obliged to explore new fields, forging new paths and adapting them to the tastes of new generations. The challenge often lies in interpreting the demands of the client (who may be excessively steeped in passing fads or commercial needs) and, subsequently, in assigning a creative value to them. Thus, in all interior design one sees an effort to strike a balance between function and aesthetics, between the essential and the non-essential.

On the following pages, you will find solutions of the most diverse types. There are, however, a handful of approaches that could be considered common to the latest preferences in contemporary interior design: a certain tendency to clear spaces of ornamental objects that obscure and blur architectural lines, the almost systematic elimination of the habitual resources used to disguise load-bearing structures, a trend toward transparent spaces with few spatial divisions, and the recurring use of light and color as integral components of the architectural solutions.

In summary, this book presents a selection of the most interesting proposals in interior design, showing a return to more humanized concepts based on the profound relationship of humankind with its inhabited space.

Arthur Collin architect
Loft Apartment in Clerkenwell

London, UK

The apartment is a single space carefully articulated with a variety of L-shaped forms. The largest 'L' is an uplighting beam that illuminates the whole space and delineates the open areas from the bathroom and foyer.

Beech wood strip flooring with galvanized steel skirting extends through most of the apartment. Wall surfaces are painted plaster or sandblasted original brickwork. The kitchen area consists of two low parallel-galvanized steel cabinets with fine-rubbed black Welsh slate tops. A planter box for herbs sits between the longer cabinet and the adjacent window. Both cabinets sit on a black slate floor. The stainless steel chimney hood over the island cabinet marks the center of this end of the apartment. The absence of other high level cabinets maintains clarity and openness.

At the opposite end of the living area is a square form lit dramatically from below. This monolith contains a wardrobe and conceals the sleeping area, which is raised slightly above the living area.

The glass mosaic-tiled bathroom is the only enclosed space and daylight floods in from the living area through a translucent glazed partition. The full height mirror opposite and the translucent glass counter top further emphasize the lightness and openness. In contrast the dark turquoise tiles of the bath and shower enclosure form a separate intimate alcove. The apartment is deceptively simple in layout but far from minimal. The imperfect nature of the repeated 'L' motif invites colonization by the inhabitants, their personality and their clutter.

The linear east7west alignment of the inserted architectural forms is offset against the three large north facing galvanized steel framed windows. This relationship orients the apartment to the city and the immediate context -the Clerkenwell area of London, which lies between The City of London and the West End.

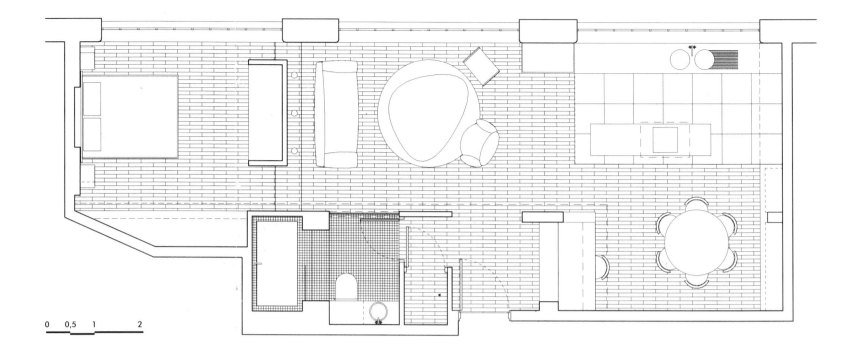

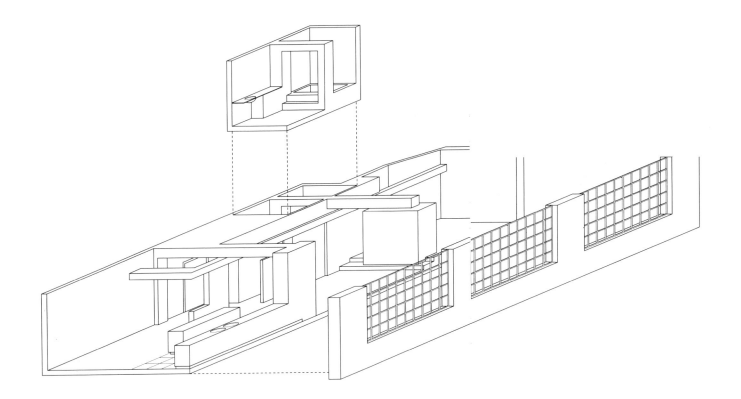

The massive use of translucent glass and mirrors in the bathroom provides lightness and the sensation of maximun opening in the only closed room of the dwelling.

5th Studio
Eden Street / Clarendon Street

Cambridge, UK

The House in the Garden of Eden was built in the mid-1800s in a former area of land known as the Garden of Eden. The project appeared at first to be concerned with the improvement of the existing single storey kitchen with bathroom beyond. As an initial investigation, the architects drew up a long term plan for moving the bathroom upstairs, the kitchen into the centre of the house and the main bedroom into a position in the garden. The client's tight budget dictated that the architects needed to institute an initial phase of work to make the house habitable and safe. The property was very poorly built and the former owner had removed the staircase.

Set perpendicularly to the former stair, which rose from the lower level of the back room to renegotiate three awkward split-levels towards the front of the house, the new stair begins in the front room and replaces much of the central division of the house. An intermediate landing formed in glass gives onto the flying-freehold room, and the future bathroom at the back of the house. A further flight rises to the front bedroom, reappearing in the front room below like a puzzle. The elision of the central structure of the house allows a top lit double height space to be formed that lights the middle of the house and emphasises the tripartite cellular and private character of "upstairs" as against the free-flowing levels of downstairs.

The Clarendon Street Project is the partial rehabilitation of a fairly typical mid-terrace Victorian house in central Cambridge. The clients had undergone an earlier remodelling of the space of the original house in the mid-1970s, but a cold and leaking back extension provided the opportunity to form a new sort of space between the house and the garden.

The existing single storey room had been built between the garden walls of the terrace. Its flat roof was leaking, and the single glazed softwood screen that formed the rear elevation at ground floor was in a poor state. The space was dark and cold.

The room mediates between the spaces of house and garden. The new space lies at the end of a ground floor plan that is bisected along the centre of the house into a kitchen and a library. Both of these twin avenues into the room are dark; the reworked space of the room is highly lit in contrast by a glass roof over half the room, and by a floor to ceiling glazed screen to the garden. The luminous quality of the garden room emphasises and makes positive the relative darkness of the library and kitchen.

The room itself is treated as two halves: the kitchen side is wholly top-lit, while the library side has a plastered soffit.

Photographs: David Grandorge

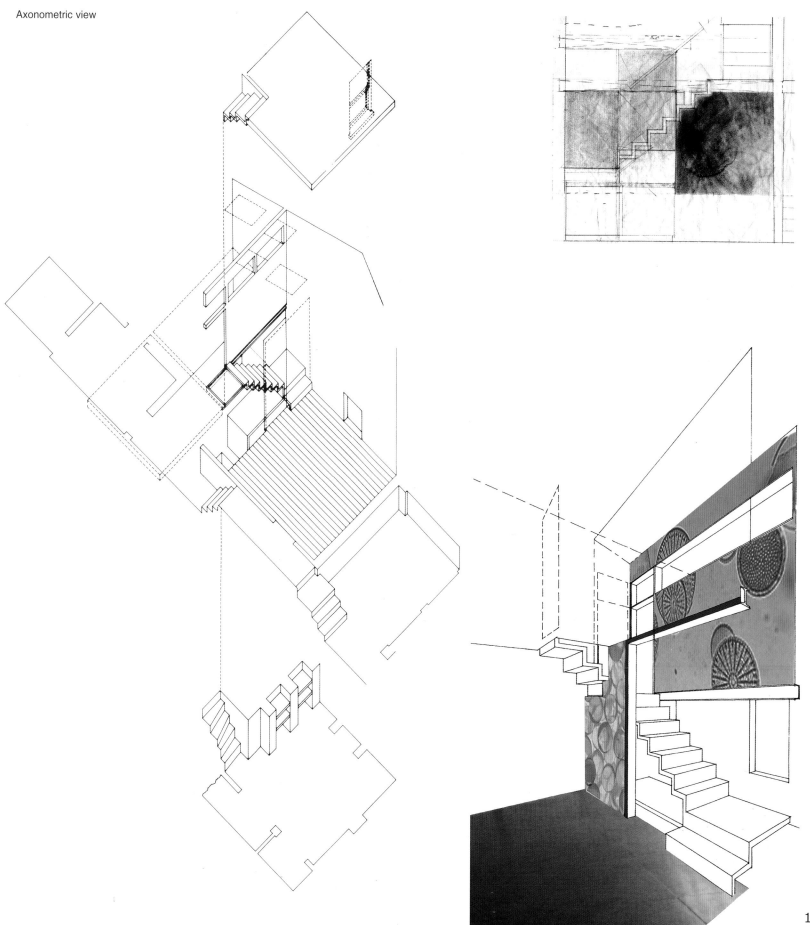

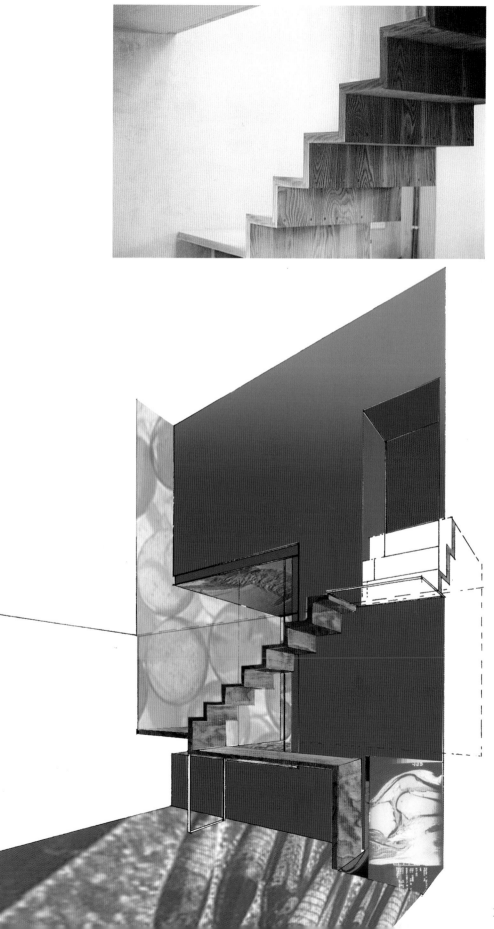

The semi-submerged cellar forces the section to rise above street level by a half storey, imposing a split-level between front and back of the house.

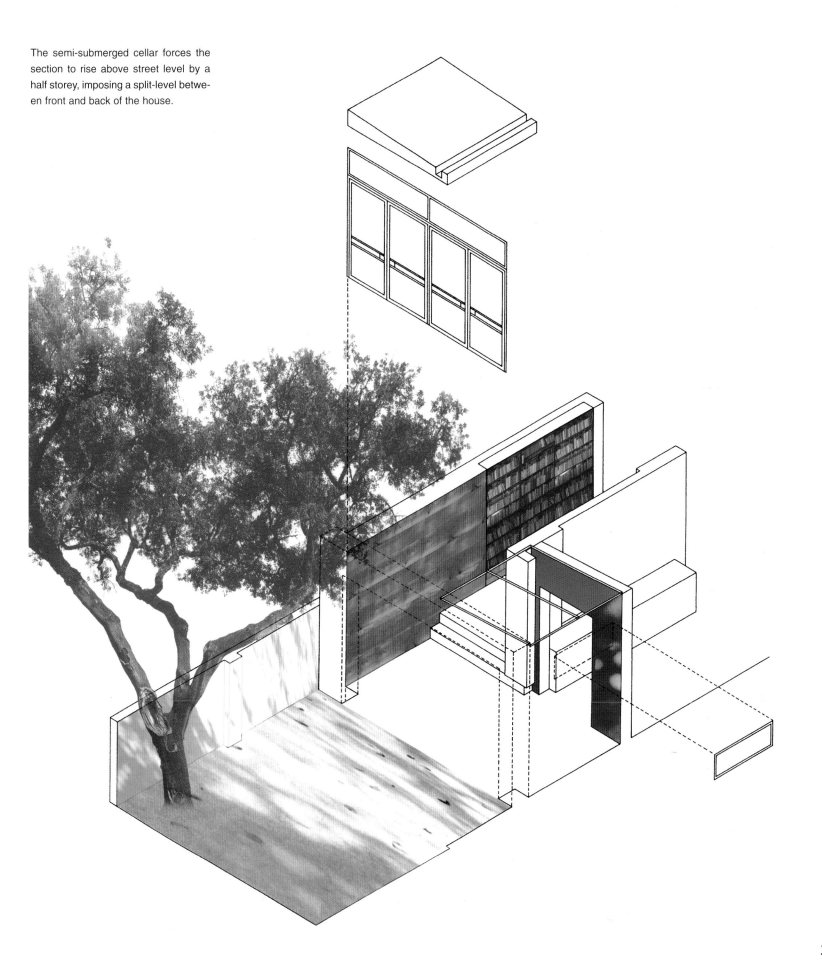

The semi-submerged cellar forces the section to rise above street level by a half storey, imposing a split-level between front and back of the house.

Werner Van dermeersch
House Arnold-Berghmans

Deurne, Belgium

The project consists of the design of a house for a family who requested three bedrooms and large open recreation areas. Known as The Golden Pavilion, the house is built in the Belgian city of Deurne, on a singular site of two pieces of land in a terrace plot ten metres wide and seventeen metres deep.

Commission requirements and local regulations made the architect design a house of thirteen meters depth, 8.50 meters height, three floors, with a flat roof and obligatory driveway leading to the second part at the rear, 12.50 metres wide and 12.50 metres deep, twisted 12º and sold as land for garages.

The shape, site and orientation of the two pieces with regard to each other formed the basis of the design.

The land at the back became the children's pavilion, entirely open to a long patio over the whole width at the rear, with the adjacent garden at the front of the building.

This volume was joined to the main house by means of a long library passage, which divides the interjacent area, passing the garden and the patio.

The main house, which occupies the whole plot at the gound level, is completely open to the garden and patio at the rear, while being entirely closed to the street at the front.

At the same time, this serves as a plinth for the parent's pavilion which stands entirely free on the first floor. This volume is seen from the exterior as a yellow cube which reveals that there is a specific function inside. The same goes for the whole complex: the geometrical composition is decorated by means of the color which describes outwardly the internal homelife rhythm.

Photographs:Jan Verlinde

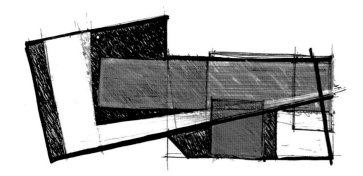

The rooms located on the ground floor were conceived as open spaces organized around a large inner courtyard.

The area of the dwelling containing the parents' room is located on the upper floor. If necessary it can be completely isolated from the rest.

Patrick Genard & Ass.
House T

Barcelona, Spain

The rehabilitation of this tower with a garden involved an interesting exercise of transmutation of polarities: tradition-modernity; culture-nature; minimalism-baroque style…

The final result is therefore the product of these opposing elements, but also of their transcendence in the search for an unstable point of balance. The volumes and composition of the facade were entirely conserved by the architects due to the planning regulations, but they treated it graphically and in two rather than three dimensions, replacing the relief elements with recessed joints. In the interior, the volumes were also respected but given fluidity by all types of visual transparencies. A space of double height was thus opened at the entrance. The stairwell was eliminated, opening many dynamic perspectives, and transparent partitions were created for continuity of the spaces. The ceilings were separated from the walls by means of an illuminated throat to blur the limits. The architects removed all structural elements in the space located under the roof, thus forming a large suite in the maisonette, and the transparent character of the rooms was enhanced by means of the repeated use of doors, sliding walls and spiral staircases of translucent glass. The architects also attempted to merge the minimalism of the layout with a certain "baroque style" in the natural materials, chosen for their strong personality and their great decorative power.

This whole endeavour is sustained though great care in the geometry and proportions and a harmonic composition of ranges of materials, from the furniture and the details to the construction itself and the works of art. These were chosen during the project in an interesting dialogue with its aesthetics, following the same philosophical line.

In summary, it was attempted to integrate the polarities to reach a harmonic and organic whole, to conjugate the objects in a whole in which opposites approach and resemble each other.

Photographs: Eugeni Pons

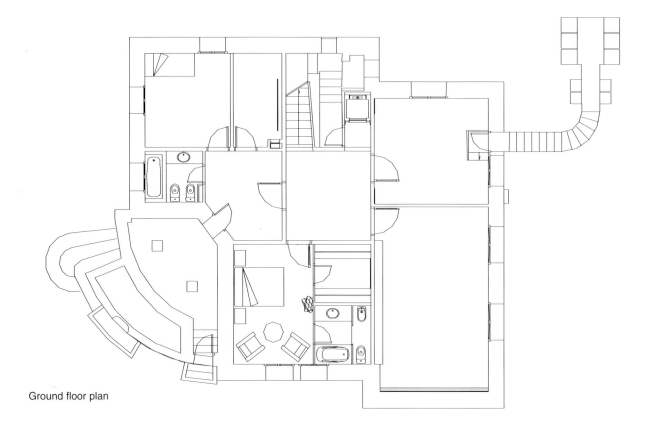

Ground floor plan

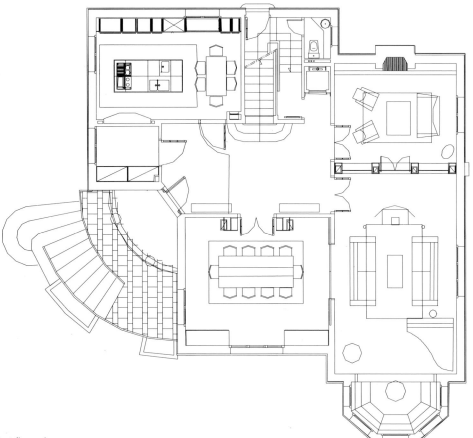

First floor plan

In the rehabilitation of this dwelling, one of the main aims was to create different spatial atmospheres in which the continuity was not interrupted by too many visual barriers. In the living room, a translucent partition and a sliding glass door that communicates with the dining room help the natural light to filter toward the interior.

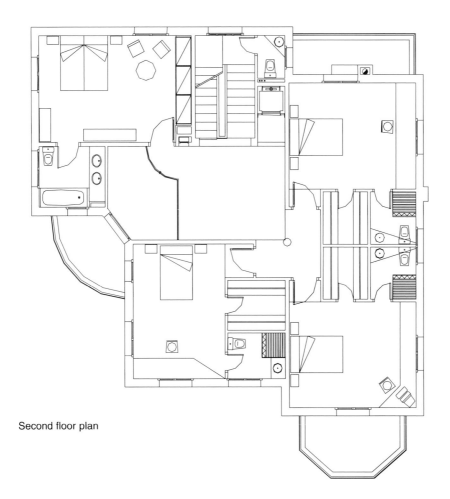

Second floor plan

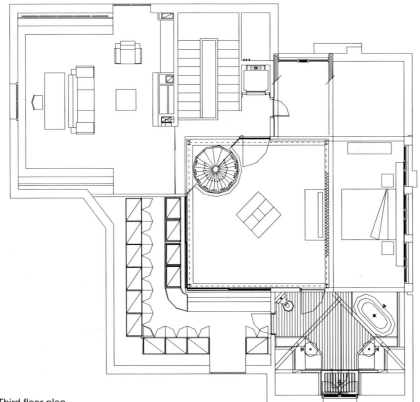

Third floor plan

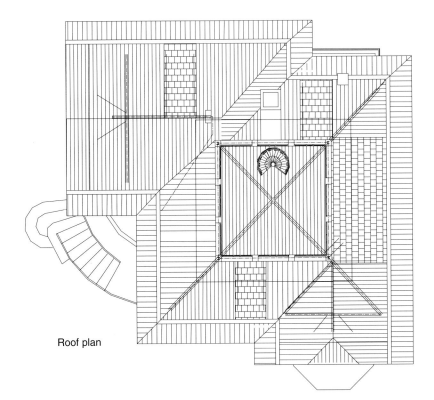

Roof plan

In order to emphasise the contrasts it was decided to combine cold and warm materials. Thus, modern glass balustrades cohabit with wooden elements, and a white, slightly veined marble is incrusted in the furniture of the dining room.

To give more personality to the different spaces and to play with the contrast chromatically, different colours were chosen for the stucco walls. In the kitchen, the combination of blue and stainless steel breaks the predominant ivory colour in the dwelling.

Details, such as the use of Portoro marble with golden veins on an ebony background for the fireplace and an oak cabinet with 48 drawers similar to Rubick's cube located in the bedroom, give final touches to the rooms.

Marco Savorelli Architects
Apartament in Milan

Milano, Italy

This is a project in which the historical memory of the site meets with a rigorous formal research, a well-balanced experimentation with the new spaces preserves the existing quality of light.

The result is a playful alternation of volumes and moods, a fluid exchange between the existing and the designed space.

These are characteristics of a project which involved from the intense dialogue between the architect and the client, aiming to achieve a minimalist aesthetics and at the same time volumetric and functional complexity. This is not a mere operation of interior decoration but the creation of volumes to be lived in and to "live with" in a completely modern and innovative way.

The space acquires both a jocose and a reflexive quality.

When entering this apartment the visual impact is instantaneous -a nearly flash-like perception of the space- which reveals the equilibrium between matter and light. The natural daylight traces delicate designs on the neat surfaces, shadows in perpetual movement creating a simple and primordial play of light.

photographs: Matteo Piazza

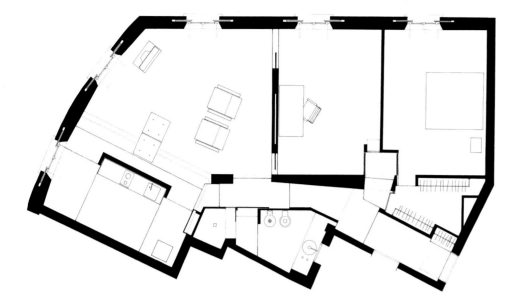

General floor plan

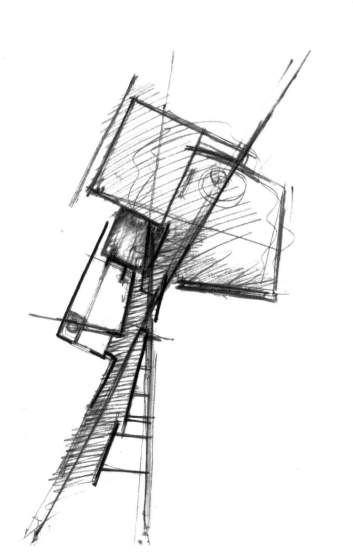

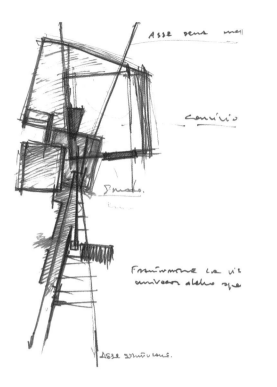

The project is a subtle combination of maximum geometric and
functional complexity with aesthetic minimalism and spatial balance.

Views of the bedroom. A folding wooden panel, which is painted in the same color as the walls to camouflage its presence, closes the entrance to the room or to the large dressing room according to its position..

Eligio Novello Arch EPFL
House Troesch-Tschan

Epalinges / Switzerland

The plot of this house is located in a new estate of single-family dwellings in Epalinges, a location of the Swiss Canton of Vaud. The simple form of the house with its clearly structured facades seems unobtrusive in the midst of the heterogeneous surrounding development, a calm refuge in the middle of a mixed area.

Using prefabricated structural timber elements, the superstructure was erected over the concrete basement in a very short time.

The external appearance is determined by the facade cladding of untreated cedar wood panels, which receive a noble grey colouring through weathering. On the south side, horizontal wood louvres form screening and solar shading both for the corridor and the entrance to the garden on the ground floor. Eventhought the very small openings on the walls, the theme of transparency was studied as a way to subtly relate the internal and external environment.

Due to the sloping site, the building is slightly raised to the east so that the terrace built there projects freely over the ground.

At the west end, the basement wall is drawn up high above ground level to support the internal staircase. The cedar-veneered fibreboard (MDF) steps with flush-sunk rubber strip are bound by four steel plates cantilevered from the wall. The angular, saw-tooth profile of the steps is brought out to striking effect, combining with the exposed concrete joints, the heating element and the horizontal balustrades to form a composition that shapes the space like a sculpture.

The project of this house won the Award in Architecture by the Canton of Vaud, 1996

Photographs: François Bertin

Eventhought the very small openings on the walls, the theme of transparency was studied as a way to subtly relate the internal and external environment.

The structure of the dwelling is shown in the interior through the exposed concrete joints.

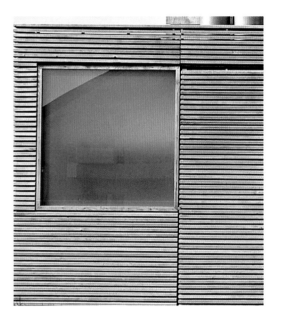

The photographs on this double page show views of the bedrooms and the bathroom located on the upper floor.

Ottorino Bersilli & Cecilia Cassina
Ristrutturazione in Manerbio

Brescia, Italy

The house is set at the end of a closed alley inside the urban fabric of Manerbio. It had long been uninhabited and used exclusively for storing material and equipment by a local building firm.

The poor condition of the building and the inappropriate intervention on part of the portico in the sixties did not curb the imagination of the new owners, helped and stimulated by the considerable dimensions of the courtyard and the garden. The fascinating volumes and the need for a clear solution to the disastrous intervention of the sixties suggested the idea of proposing a sequence of recognizable architectural elements on both the façades. The original brickwork of the portico was revealed, the stone wall was cleaned and the wooden roof structure was rebuilt.

The three-storey house of the early 20th century was recovered with the typical structure of the epoch, a stone staircase leading to the different levels and dividing each floor into two rooms.

The central body from the sixties acts as an element of union and dates the intervention.

On the facade of the extremely rational cube, the evidence of the sequence of the pillars of the portico suggested the form of the openings, which at nighttime turn the interior spaces into a permeable and transparent box.

The organic nature of the materials and the almost obsessive repetition of a single color (floors, masonry, frames) conflict strongly with the wing of the laundry and kitchen in blood red and with the wall and the pillar of the living room in exposed brickwork.

The new distributive order stimulates the use of the whole residence, giving precedence to certain parts over others according to the seasons. For example, in winter the large living room of the first floor is giving preference, whereas in summer the outer zone giving onto the garden is used more.

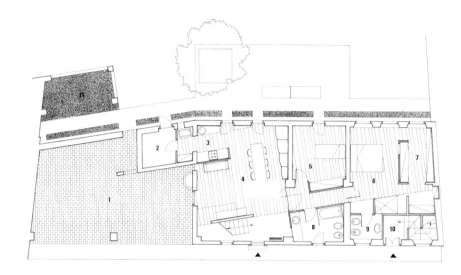

Ground floor plan

Views of the kitchen area and dining room located on the lower level. These rooms are separated from the bedrooms by means of a fitted wardrobe that has curved metal doors with a matte finish and a swiveling door.

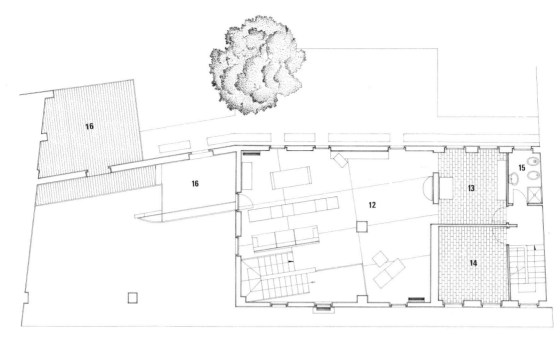

First floor plan

The two-flight staircase communicating the ground floor with the upper level is made of colored, reinforced cement to which thin steel bars have been attached as a handrail.

On this page, several views of the living area located on the upper floor. This communicates with the external terrace that looks onto the garden through a small balcony and a walkway anchored to the stone wall.

Waro Kishi & K. Associates
House in Shimogamo

Kyoto, Japan

This two-storey house is located in an urban area at the foot of the Kitayama Mountains in the northern part of Kyoto. Covering almost the entire plot, the house has a frontage 3.2 m x 2 spans and a depth of 4 m x 3 spans. At the core of the steel-frame structure, the architect has created a nakaniwa (inner court) measuring 2 m x 3 spans. The rest of the house consists of a steel frame with exterior walls made of formed cement plates, steel sashes, and large doors. Designing this house, Kishi was fully aware that a contemporary urban house could only convey a sense of reality as a one-off solution to a number of fixed preconditions. At the same time, however, he made an attempt to realize the kind of prototype urban house, that has been a dream of 20th century modernism. He thus focused on incorporating new ideas into planning and structure, which are the most important aspects of modern architecture.

In designing the house, it was not his main intention to secure privacy. Instead the architect placed emphasis on the relationship between the exterior space - that is, the nakaniwa - and the rooms facing it. The result is a large three-dimensional one-room living space, with individual rooms that are independent yet mutually interrelated. Nor did he give preference to the structure. Rather, he considered it as a part of the overall assembly of basic elements, to achieve the impression of a single functional unit. After all, several decades after the mythological age of modern architecture the time may have come to re-think the architecture of the machine age.

photographs: Hiroyuki Hirai

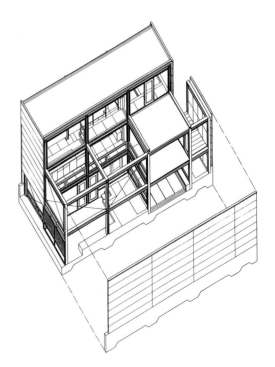

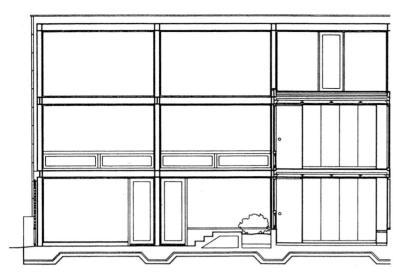

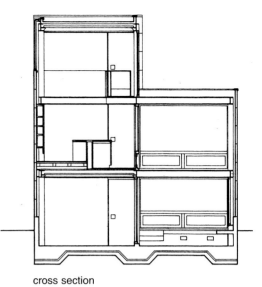

Longitudinal section

cross section

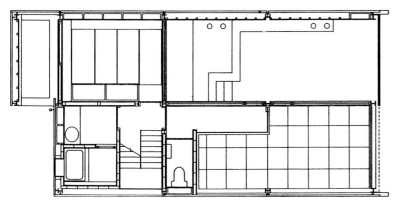

Ground floor plan

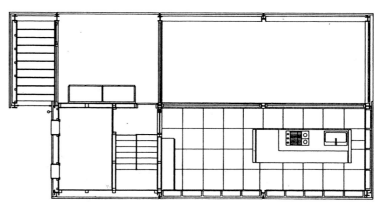

First floor plan

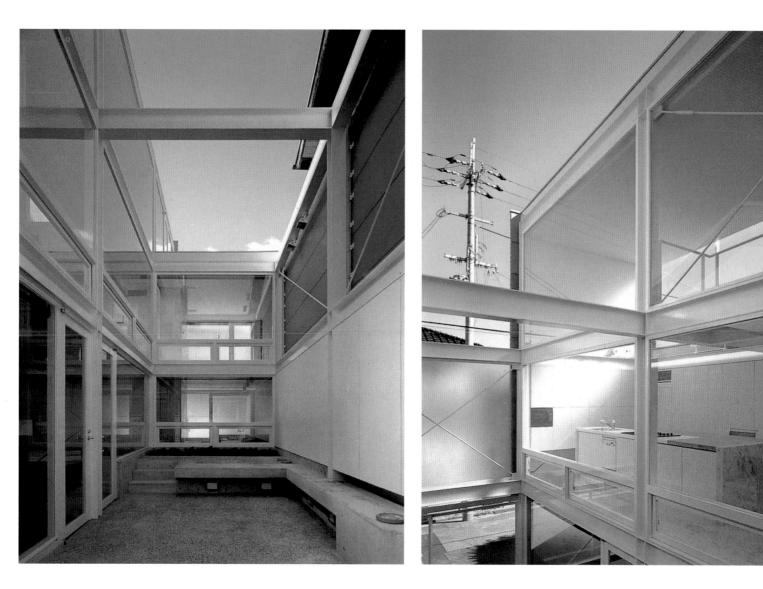

The three-dimensional structure, treated as just another element of the building, gives unity to the functional units of the dwelling.

Despite the extreme simplicity of the forms and the small number of materials used, the écheme achieves great spatial and volumetric quality.

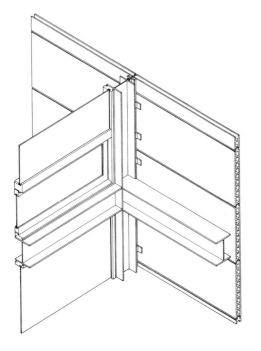

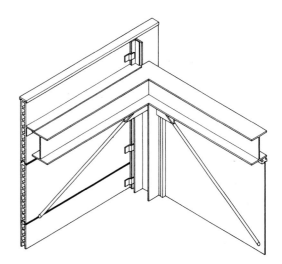

Koh Kitayama
Omni Quarter

Tokyo, Japan

This multi-purpose building, which is located in one of Tokyo's most sophisticated areas, has a basement floor, which houses an atelier, and four stories, covering a total floor area of 863m². Living quarters are on the third and fourth floors; a shop occupies the first and second floors.

A spacious, atrium-like space has been annexed onto the south side. This space serves the dual purpose of providing a stairwell which does not obstruct the central living space and an air layer that is part of a double-skin environmental control device.

This latter function is part of the architects' philosophy of designing structures which handle environmental conditions in a more rational manner: it is the inhabitants who decide when their home needs a "change of clothes", opening and closing household fixtures in response to the given climate and season.

This building also displays a characteristic which is not only typical of this studio's work, but to Asian house architecture in general: a planar format, with hallways and stairways placed at the periphery of the living area, thereby creating spaces which are easily adaptable to changes in daily living.

The building is an equal span rigid-frame structure with support columns on the inside, which frees up space in the hallways.

Photographs: Nobuaki Nakagawa

Feeling that Japanese architecture has tended in the past several years toward sterile and homogenous spaces, this studio sought a more "user-friendly" design. All skylights and openings can be opened or closed according to the season or weather conditions.

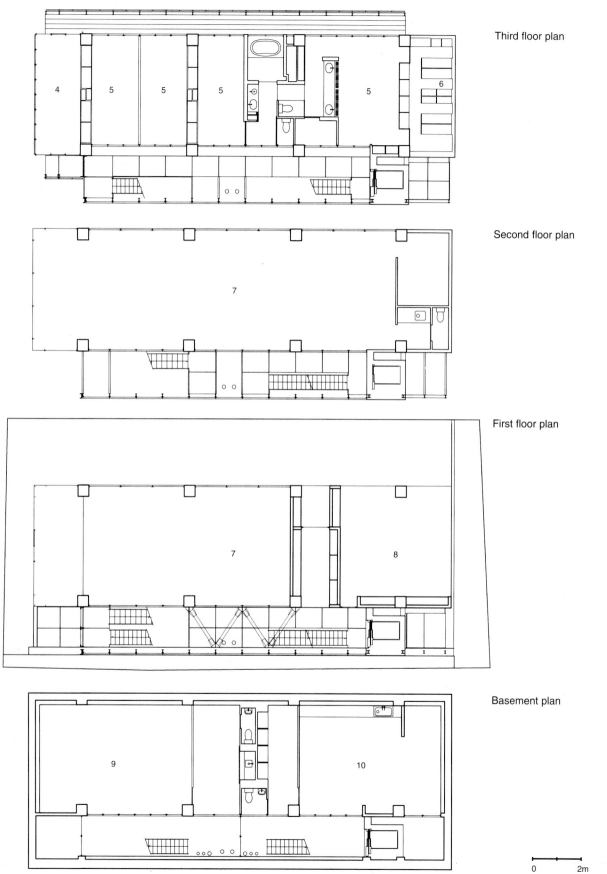

Third floor plan

Second floor plan

First floor plan

Basement plan

0   2m

1. Work space
2. Pantry
3. Multi-use room
4. Atelier
5. Private room
6. Cloak
7. Tenant
8. Parking area
9. Gallery
10. Ceramics atelier

Fourth floor plan

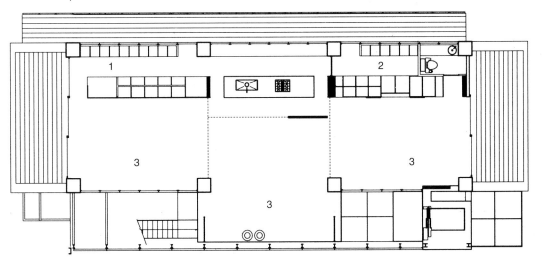

The building is an equal span, rigid-frame structure, which has provided ample space on the periphery for communication routes, thereby freeing the living area from obstructions.

Sergio Calatroni
Gallery Uchida

Milan, Italy

The project consists in rehabilitating a 90m² space situated in the city of Milan, in order to adapt it and convert it into a gallery dwelling.

The gallery, in which works of art by the owner of the dwelling are exhibited, is on the first level. This floor are also houses the kitchen and a small bathroom, whereas the whole of the upper floor is taken up by the bedroom and the main bathroom. The lower floor communicates through large French windows with a terrace that provides the space with light.

The whole project is articulated by means of fixed and mobile walls. The kitchen and the bathroom on the lower floor are separated from the gallery by means of a movable panel. The geometric finishes of this panel were made by combining white, black and reddish wood. The floor, a magnificent surface of cherry wood, brings unity to the dwelling.

A minimalist staircase of folded sheet leads to the upper floor where the bedroom is located. The two-toned sculptural element that divides the staircase and also performs the function of a banister was made in Greek-work sheet.

photographs: Sergio Calatroni

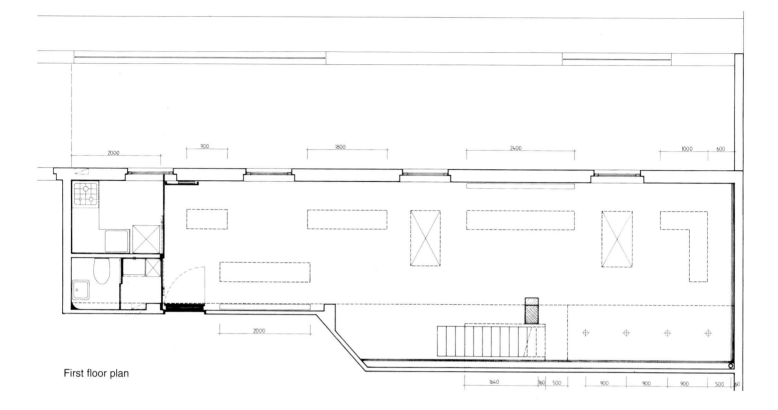

First floor plan

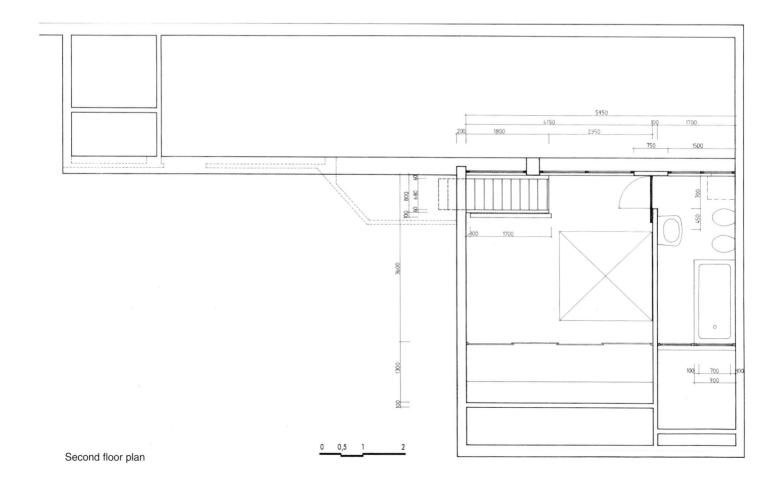

Second floor plan

0   0,5   1   2

Cross section

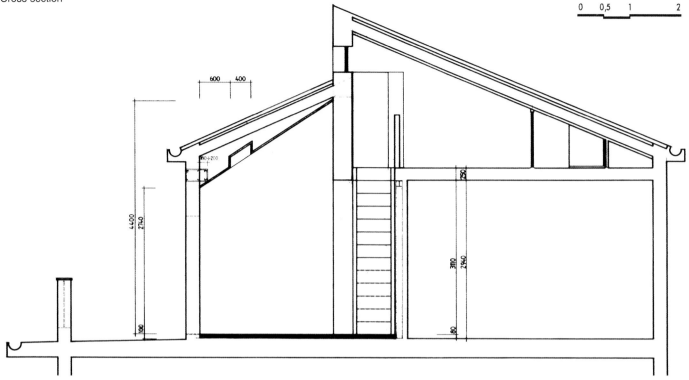

Longitudinal sections of the bathroom

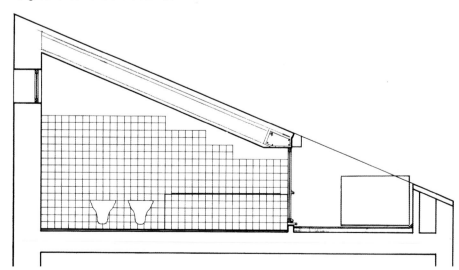

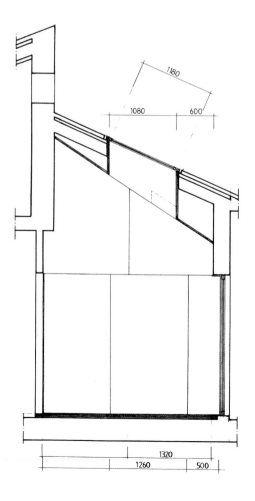

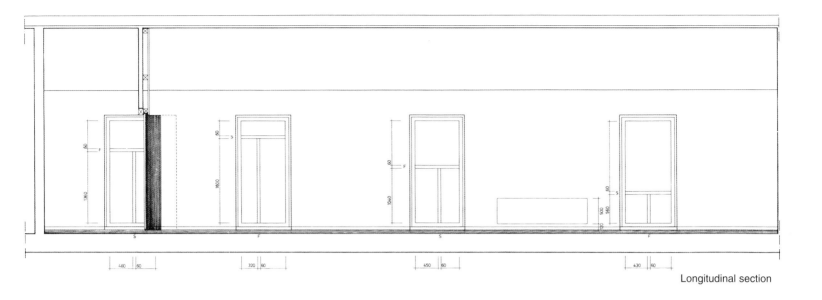

Longitudinal section

Construction detail of the window

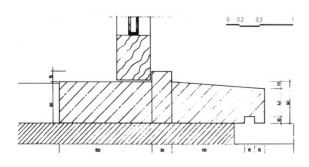

Bruce Kuwabara & Evan Webber
Residence and Studio in Richmond Hill

Ontario, Canada

The design of the Reisman-Jenkinson Residence and Studio combines living and working spaces for a family of four in the suburban context of Richmond Hill, Ontario.

Four buildings constructed of light-grey, split faced concrete blocks are joined by three glazed linking elements to create a forecourt and garden courtyard.

Shaped roof elements on the sculpture studio and main living building are fabricated from anodized, formed aluminum panels. Fascias, coverings and cuppers complete each building and linking element.

The sculpture studio forms one edge of the forecourt. The interior receives indirect north light through clerestory windows.

A pair of doors constructed of Douglas fir open out onto the courtyard, framing views of a spectacular landscape of silver maple trees.

The conservatory entrance forms the opposite edge of the forecourt and connects the studio and main loft buildings. Simple volumes, high ceilings, large windows and door openings, and maple hardwood floors create the feel of a loft building. Fireplaces anchor the two ends of the living loft, while a pyramidal skylight establishes the kitchen space as a kind of third internal courtyard.

Bedrooms and writing studios are grouped around the landscaped garden courtyard. Large sliding panels in the main loft and master bedroom buildings adjust the degree of privacy to create a flexible living arrangement.

In this work, architecture supports a vision of an alternative lifestyle in the suburbs. The design challenges conventional expectations about domesticity and celebrates the parallel existence of artistic practices and the rituals of daily life.

photograhs: Steven Evans

Site plan

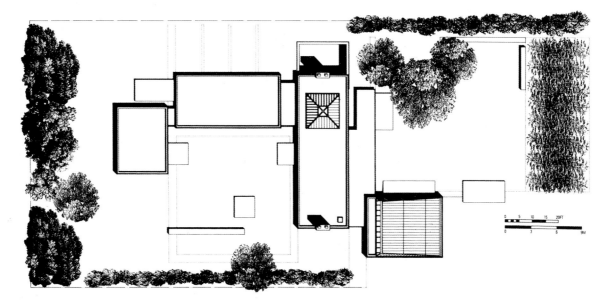

This design creates four small volumes that are interconnected through the use of glass elements, thereby creating a series of exterior patios.

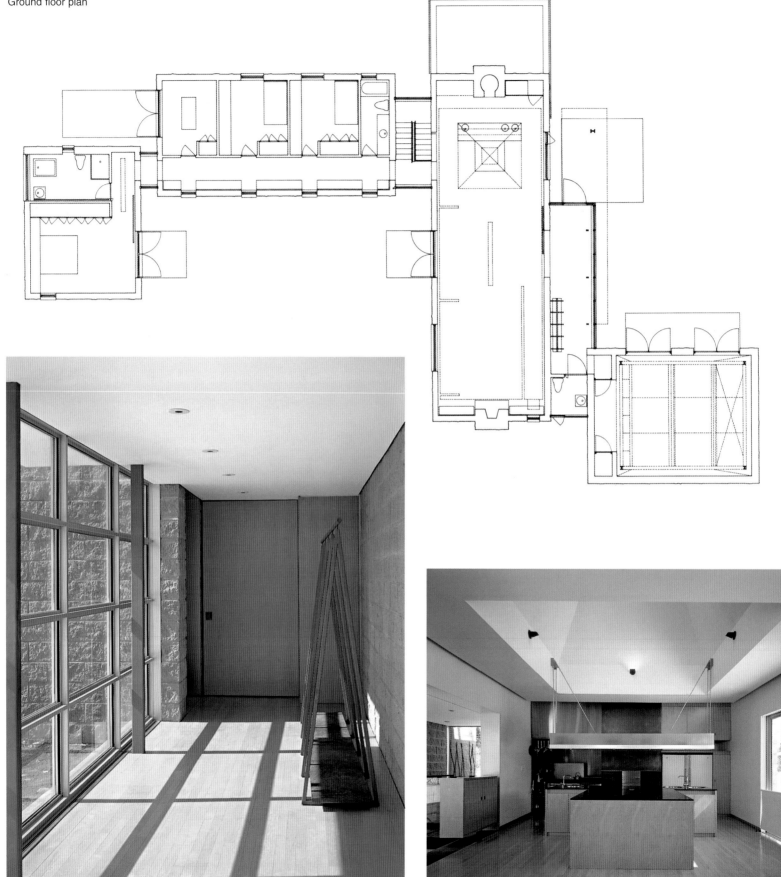

The maple-wood floor is an eye-catching feature of the interior, contrasting with the simple plastered walls..
The living-dining room area runs parallel to the street. The only notable furnishing element is the spacious kitchen located in a central position of the room.

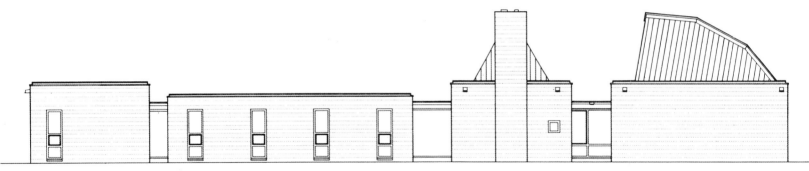

West elevation

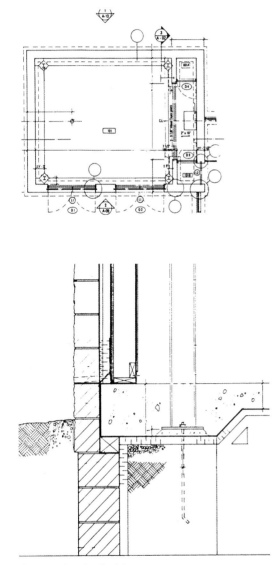

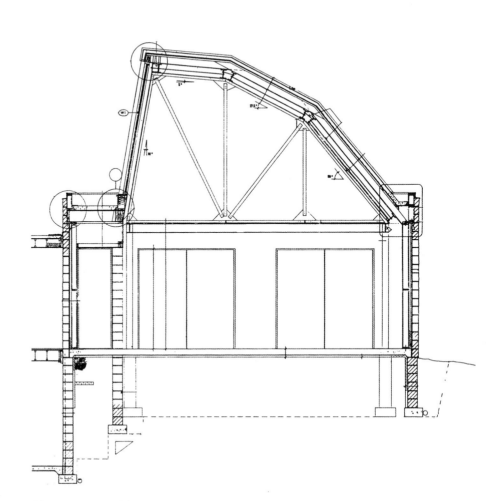

Construction detail of the garage

Plan and section of the garage

Valerio Dewalt Train
Gardner Residence

Chicago, USA

From the very beginning of modern times in America, the traditions of European architecture have undergone an important and symbolic transformation. The substantial elements of traditional design were replaced with architecture of increasing thinness - everything which was substantial became lighter and almost weightless. Thin stud walls of wood and plywood replaced the thick substantial wall of stone and mansory. The Gardner Residence extends this trend to its ultimate conclusion.

The "site" is on the 58th and 59th floor of a Michigan Avenue high rise, and is dominated by the looming dark mass of the John Hancock Tower to the north. The apartment is divided between "ceremonial" and "functional" spaces. In the beginning the apartment was considered as a single space within the enclosing walls. In this space, two idealized boxes were inserted: one of metal, one of wood, one on the first level, the other on the second. These containers define the ceremonial space within the apartment. Each box is impos-

sibly thin, composed of just barely enough substance to retain their form.

In homage to the John Hancock Building, each box is warped by the Tower's imagined gravitational pull. The aluminum shell is defined by a series of straight lines, which are orthogonal either to the city grid or the angled sides of the Tower. The curves of the wood shell are tangential to an imagined circle passing through the four outer corners of the Tower.

The leftover space between the walls of these new containers and the outer apartment walls provide the bare minimum of space for the messy, problematic activities of sleeping, cooking, bathing and storage. The details evolved from these basic concepts. Almost every surface of each container is hinged providing access to the different functional areas. The stair to the second floor is so thin it defies explanation. The TV area is both idealized and functional. It has been attached to one of the pivoting metal panels where it functions as part of both the sleeping and bathing area.

photographs: Barbara Karant

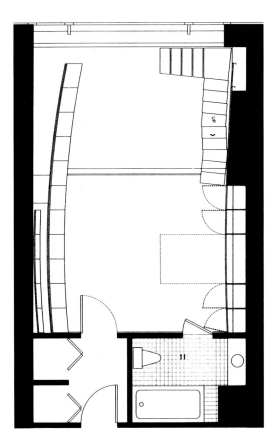

In the interior of the apartment, the space is arranged around two intersecting boxes: a horizontal one on the lower floor housing the living area, and a vertical one on the upper floor housing the study. The space that is common to the two boxes houses the bathroom and kitchen.

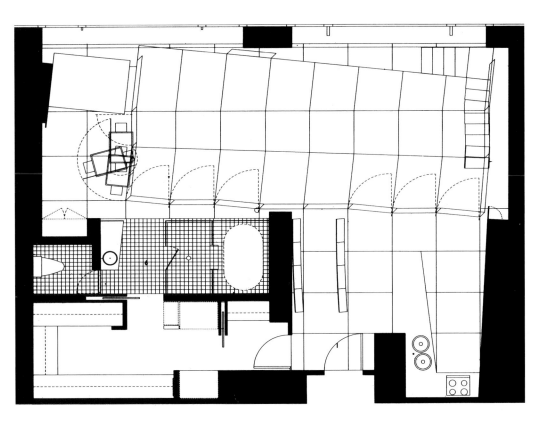

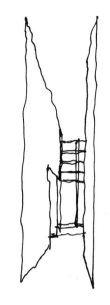
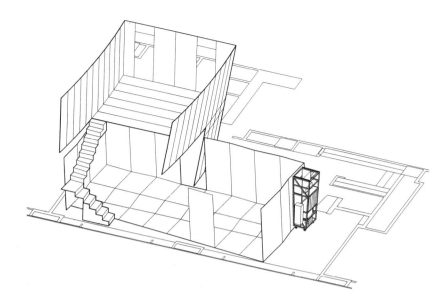

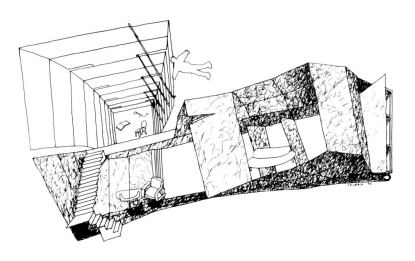

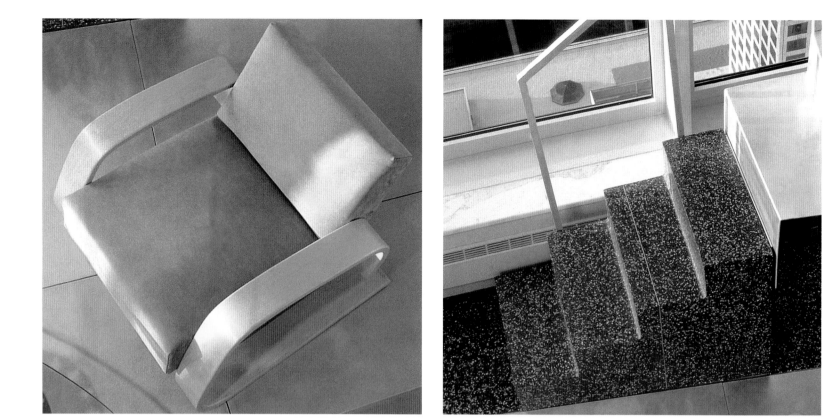

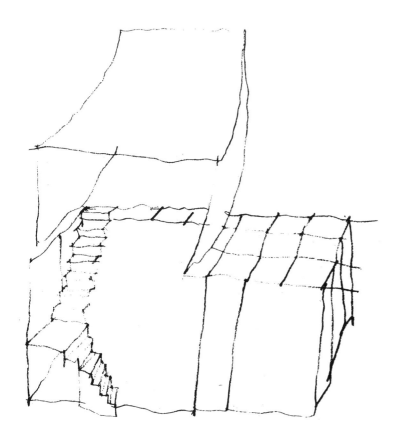

Koh Kitayama
Plane + House

Tokyo, Japan

This house, with an attached studio and a total floor area of 177m², occupies almost the entirety of its small plot, located in a densely populated area of Tokyo. The client is an industrial designer who required that the building include facilities for both a home and office.

Because of local zoning restrictions the construction area is an exact square, which at least offers the possibility of creating wide-open, diaphanous spaces. The building is an equal span rigid-frame structure with supporting columns on the inside, freeing up space in the hallways. The space formed between the outer and inner walls is used for staircases, and also serves as a ventilation duct. Top-lit glass has been installed in the ceiling in this space, guiding natural light downwards.

This structure displays the planar format of homes often seen in Asia, with hallways running around the outside of the living areas. Such spaces are easily adaptable to changes in daily living.

However, in other aspects, the architects have consciously tried to distance the design of this biulding from typical Japanese architecture. They feel that in the past several years, particularly in Japan, there has been a trend towards an almost unnatural sterility and homogeneity, reminiscent of the brightly-lit convenience store equipped with air conditioning and heating. Homes in which spatial composition and environment-friendly technology support one another are not —but perhaps shoud be— the norm. As a response, they have designed a home in which the occupants must recognize when it is time for a "change of clothes", opening and closing household fixtures according to the given climate and season.

Photographs: Nobuaki Nakagawa

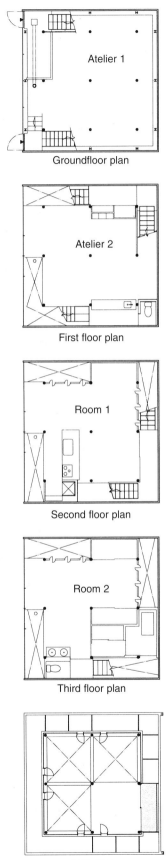

Groundfloor plan

Atelier 1

First floor plan

Atelier 2

Second floor plan

Room 1

Third floor plan

Room 2

Loft plan

Section

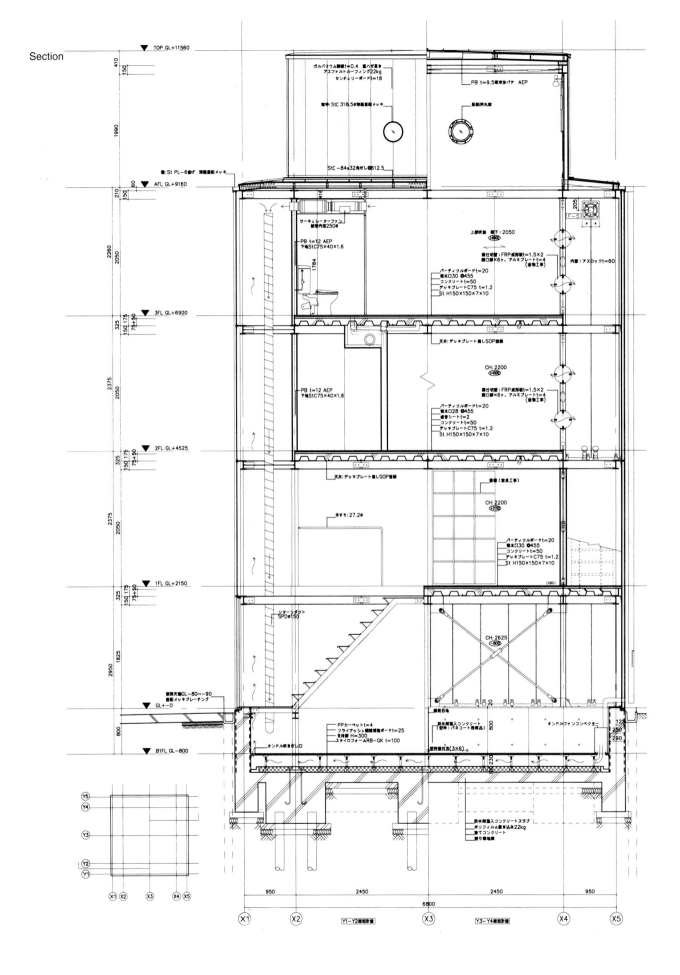

Due to zoning laws, the construction space is an exact square, a limitation which nonetheless gave rise to the creation of wide-open spaces. Hallways and stairways have been placed on the periphery of the living areas.

Harry Seidler & Associates
Farrell House

Sydney, Australia

This house for a family with two teenage boys is built on a suburban site with an oblique view toward Sydney Harbor.

The typologically very original parti shows a construction at the same time turned in on itself around the spiral staircase and strongly connected to the exterior by the striking projection of the curved balcony of prestressed concrete, glass and metal.

The house is curved in the direction of the view, the living room and master bedroom opening over it. The opposing view to the rear is over the garden, dominated by a huge eucalyptus. The ground slopes up from the street, locating the main floor on a level with the garden, over which the family room opens to reveal the swimming pool, built against the back boundary.

The focal point of the house is the spiral staircase, with its large overhead skylight, around which the corridorless plan revolves. In order to maintain a visually transparent environment, the living room, family room, dining room and study and guestroom are separated by glass walls and doors.

The upper floor contains four bedrooms, each with private bathroom, while the ground floor houses the entrance hall, double garage and playroom.

The edges of the concrete floors are expressed on the exterior, projecting down over ribbon windows. The walls are of concrete blocks specially formulated to expose selected aggregate on their polished exterior.

All outdoor glass is installed without any framing, even the curved sliding doors being of toughened glass. Protection from the sun is provided by vertical aluminum blades bracketed to the structural supports.

Photographs: Eric Sierins

104

The finish of the specially formulated concrete blocks, polished to show the gravel and other materials of which it is comprised, contrasts with the clean cut of the aluminum and glass.

The two opposing quadrants cut off the corners of the square plan of the house. The most handsome effect is achieved in the balance between the flat surface of the facade and its dominating curve.

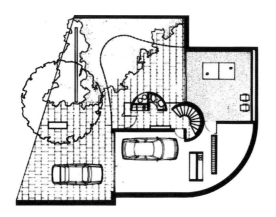

Ground floor plan

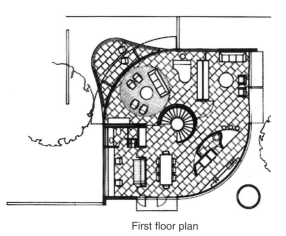

First floor plan

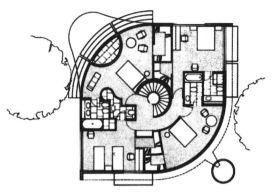

Second floor plan

The glass and concrete of the balcony creates a highly theatrical effect at night.

The positioning of the staircase and the abundance of transparent spaces around it spotlights this feature and endows it with a scenographic quality.

Randy Brown
Study Residence in Omaha

Nebraska, USA

This building includes the studio of three architects and the dwelling of one of them, Randy Brown with his wife, Kim. The building dates from the late seventies and was originally a nursery school.

It is a 40 x 40 foot cube and opens onto the environment through large south-facing windows protected by louvers and awnings. Located in Dodge Street, one of the busiest arteries of Omaha, the building is still a powerful presence in the streetscape and it would be difficult to guess its use as an office, if it were not for a small wooden panel indicating its function at the entrance. When the Browns bought the old school, it was clearly in a phase of deterioration. They designed and rehabilitated the building while living in it. The only room that they finished before moving in was the shower.

With this working method, the interior is conceived as a living entity that is undergoing constant metamorphosis. As Brown reveals, it was a good experiment to experience directly all the problems characteristic of the process of architectural work. Also, it helped to see more clearly the short-comings and real needs of the space as they went along. The space can be continually changed or reconstructed for diverse uses. The site is large, which favors the possibility of future extensions or raising a new building next to the existing one. The exterior spaces will be developed in the form of courtyards and gardens. The work process was as follows: the original building was "cleaned" of extras until it was a white shell.

The exterior was then considered ready to incorporate all the functional elements (external staircases, walls, handrails, etc.). The interior perimeter walls were left white as surfaces for hanging the plans made in the studio.

The heart of the building was occupied by a container-structure that gives the interior of the dwelling a powerful personality. It is a collage of wood, metal and glass that forms several elements (bookshelves, wall, dressing room, closet, glass table) and creates a common space on the ground floor (dining room/meeting room) and the bedroom on the first floor. This sculptural element also serves to divide the ground floor into two environments. On the left of the entrance is the studio area, on the right several spaces of the dwelling, although they are also shared by the employees of the studio: the kitchen, the bathroom and a small storeroom.

photographs: Farshid Assassi

Site plan

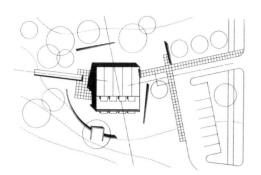

Ground floor plan

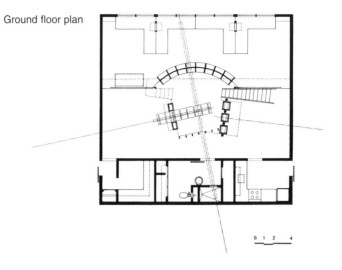

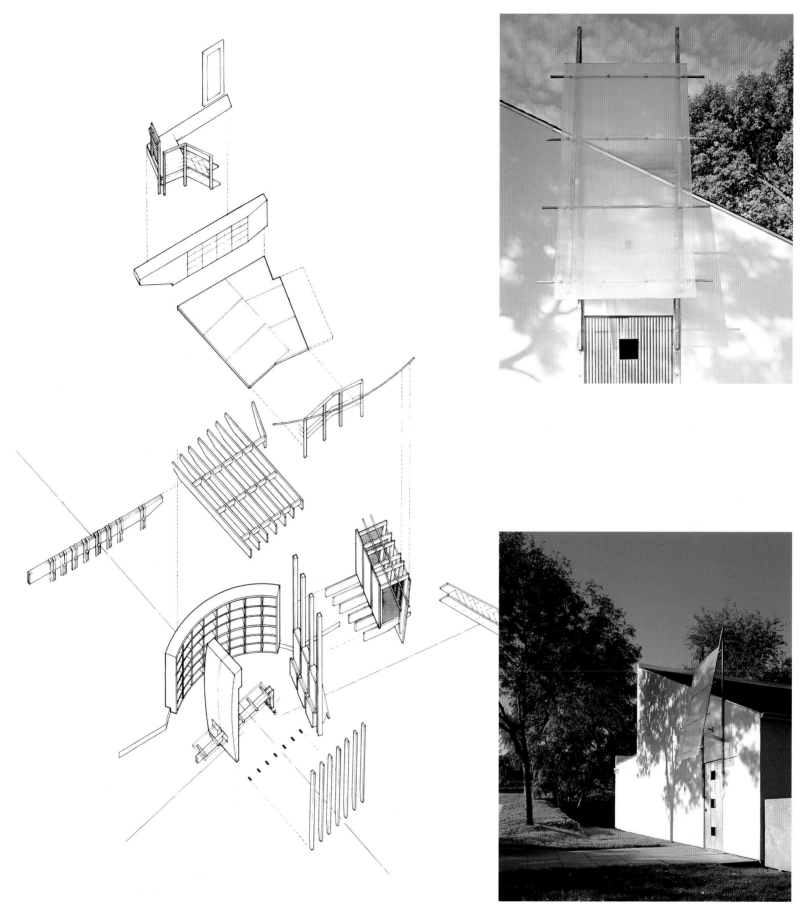

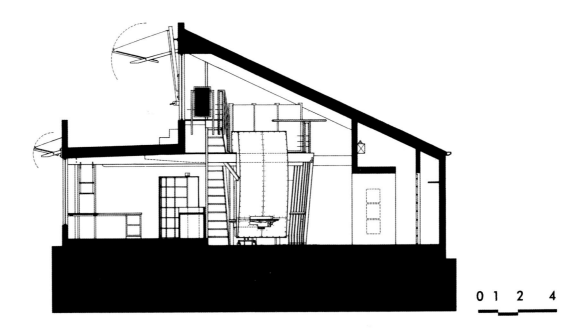

0 1 2 4

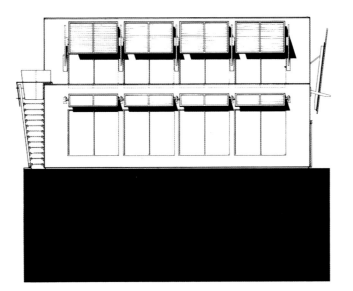

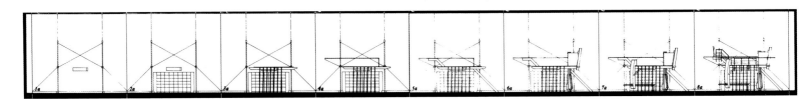

114

The lightness of the structures and materials used will make future modifications of the interior of the building easier.

The linearity and symmetry of the perimetral spaces contrasts with the volumetric solidity of the central area of the building.

The upper floor of the building houses the rest area, which also provides a direct access to the roof.

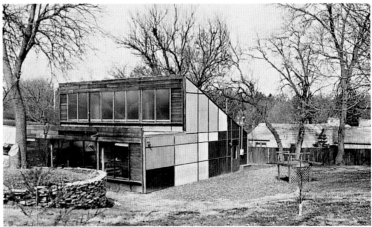

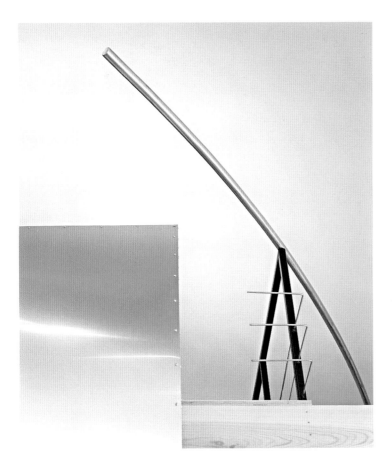

The storage element located in the centre of the floor provides a physical and visual connection between the two levels.

Dieter Thiel

Bangert Studio and House

Schopfheim, Germany

This German publisher's office on the slopes of an old orchard in the Black Forest is made of wood in the traditional way, but is entirely modern in design, technology and ecological awareness. The two buildings, while sharing the site with a house from the 50s, are completely divorced from it and each other and positioned in relation to some fine mature trees. They are an outstanding example of future-oriented design both ecologically and structurally. They also comply with the client's desire for clearly legible timber house architecture with variable lighting conditions, excellent indoor climatisation and perfect acoustics. The major of the two new structures (studio and library) comprises three different sized "wooden boxes" arranged in open plan so that, given the complete absence of partitions, the open cluster creates a room of great visual tension 17.6 meters long and with three different widths and heights. The other new cube, rising obliquely positioned at some distance from it on a 7.2 m². floor plan functions as a two-storey guesthouse.

As opposed to conventional timber houses, its fundamental difference is that it has uncompromisingly materialized the idea of a building devoid of extra finishings such as cladding and lining. The system complied at once with the client's demand that individual cubes be prefabricated on a maximum scale to achieve the best possible quality of workmanship and the shortest possible in-situ installation time.

photographs: Klaus Frahm / Contur

Longitudinal section

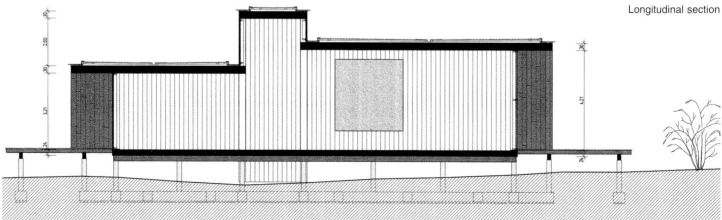

East elevation

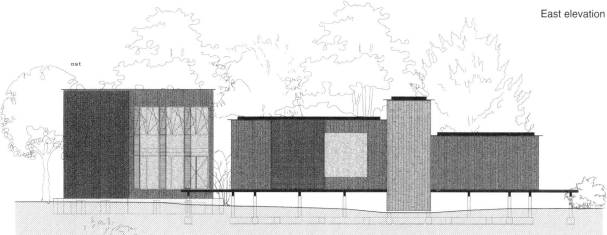

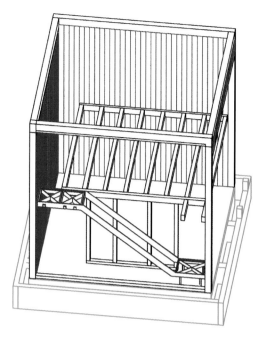

Both the interior and exterior were clad in red sequoia that does not require treatment or impregnation to withstand atmospheric conditions and biological agents.

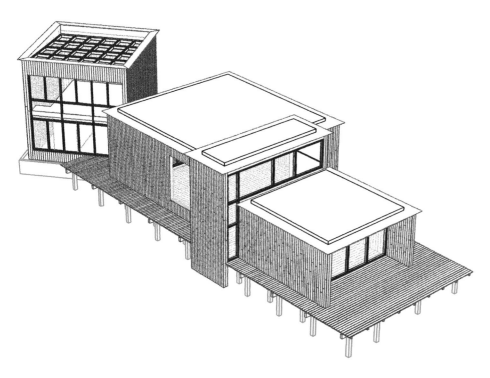

José Cruz Ovalle
Study and Home in Vitacura

Santiago de Chile, Chile

This scheme is located in a neighborhood consisting of single-family dwellings surrounded by large gardens. The area was developed fifty years ago near the river Mapocho that crosses the city of Santiago from east to west. At the present time the neighborhood has been consolidated and occupies a relatively central position in the city.

The 665-m² sites are flanked by a single-family dwelling converted into a store and another dwelling whose garden has an area of approximately one hectare. Inside it stand two separate buildings that create between them a garden-courtyard: the studio next to the street and the dwelling at the rear.

The space of the front garden is treated as a public space: it is not fenced off as is habitual in the neighborhood, so the studio has a public rather than a domestic character.

The studio is placed crossways on the site occupying the total width, so its interior space extends on two fronts: toward the street and toward the garden-courtyard of the dwelling. The interior is developed so that there is a complete and flowing perspective of the internal space from any angle - it is an interior in which to linger. This is achieved by retaining the internal void through the articulation of depth without creating a vanishing point. Wooden surfaces fold and unfold to temper the light without producing shade or glare on the work surfaces. Openings and interstices are carefully angled to receive the different types of light entering from different directions according to the time of day and the season.

On the other side, the dwelling, situated at the rear of the site facing the northern sun, opens up toward the garden-courtyard between the two buildings. The volume of the studio, located in front of the house, closes this space and prevents a vanishing point toward the street.

It is habitual in Santiago to enter houses from the street, cross them and end up in a living room in front of the garden. This is a way of conceiving space on the basis of the direction. But in this house the order is inverted because one enters the living room from the garden.

The architect did not start from isolated directions but tried to redirect the space, managing the depth and controlling the vanishing point. Thus, for example, the arrangement of the diagonal walls in the living room and the thickness between the pillars and the plane of the windows opens a transverse depth that continues through the trees, the grass and the bushes to the facade of the studio.

Because the openings through which the light penetrates the house are much larger, dark wooden parquet was used for the horizontal plane of the floor, in order for it to absorb and control the luminosity.

With this system the furniture, the objects and the building itself do not receive the light reflected from the floor, which gives them a more solid and settled image.

photographs: Juan Purcell

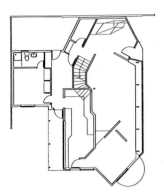

Ground floor plan

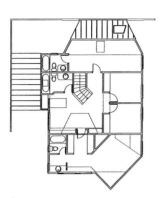

First floor plan

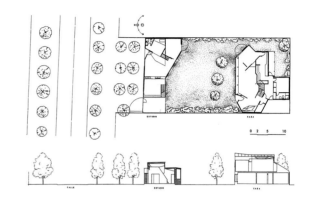

Site plan

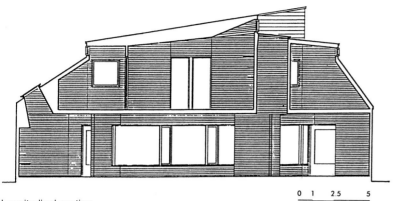

Longitudinal section

0 1 2.5 5

The tempered light is captured without reflections in the interior by means of the articulation of the pleats and folds of the wooden surfaces.

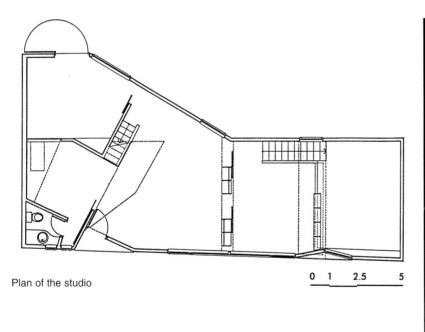

Plan of the studio

0 1 2.5 5

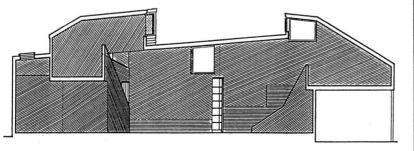

Michael Szyszkowitz & Karla Kowalski
Home Office for a Psychotherapist

Bad Mergentheim, Germany

This project -by the Austrian architects Michael Szyszcowitz and Karla Kowalsky in collaboration with Peter Kosjek and Brigitte Rathmanner- consisted of designing a family home and the consulting rooms for a psychotherapist on a steep south-facing site about 2000 m² in area.

Here too, the apparently problematic nature of a building site on a steeply sloping terrain was transformed into an advantage. The southwestern orientation, with its panoramic views and the terraced dry walls of former vineyards, were the design's point of departure. Once again, topographical peculiarities have been transformed into an expressive and original built form.

The distinctive contour of the slope became the house's major internal and external motif. The ground plan is an approximate V-shape, with the area between the two wings a secluded courtyard shaded by old trees. At the point where foundation and subsoil meet, battered buttressed walls allow the sloping terrain to merge gradually into the house's volume.

This has made it possible to plant small trees and shrubbery up to the middle storey, extending through an arbor to the roof. The low-lying roof on this side of the house rises steeply on the other side and then curves out again towards the site. Underneath this curve is the center of the house, a vaulted living room.

The house is not rendered as a fixed, traditional form, but rather as a composition of different kinds of spatial intimacy. Daylight is a specially important element in this house, and illuminates the rooms in a variety of ways. Because the light enters from four directions, the moods of the season can be enjoyed all day long.

photographs: Gert von Bassewitz

134

135

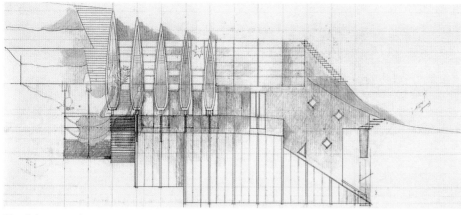

The living room is structured as a double-height space, producing a richness and spatial variety that are tempered by the presence of the curved roof.
Access to the children's rooms on the upper floor is structured as a high walkway.

Dick van Gameren & Mastenbroek
Kantoor en Penthouse

Amsterdam, The Netherlands

The project is focused on the restoration of part of three canal houses on the Keizersgracht to serve the needs of the Dutch branch of an international computer company. The office takes up the first floor of a large town house that had been created from the amalgamation of three canal houses. The original interiors have disappeared, and the breakings down of the walls and the leveling out of differences in height between the different buildings have damaged the original layout.

Additions have been treated through the position, the connections and the usage of materials as new elements that do not hide the historical body of he building.

The conversion of the office was the beginning of a plan for the total renovation of the complex. The main concerns were the improvement of the relationship with he spacious back garden (designed by Mien Ruys) and the addition of a number of bedroom and a second kitchen.

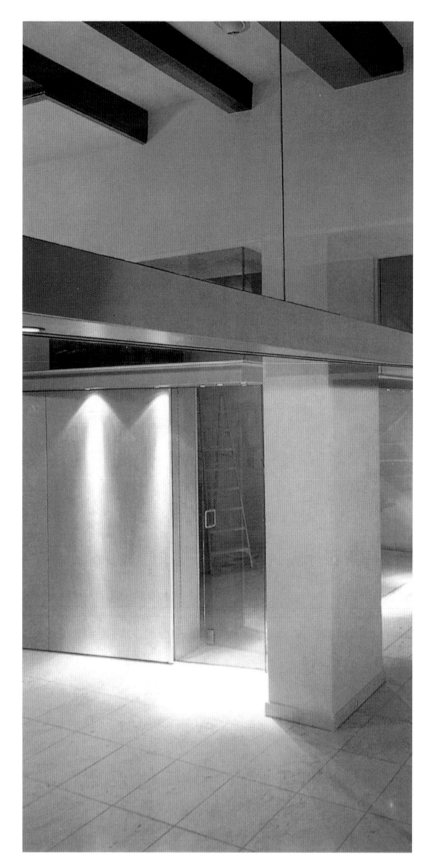

The construction of a rooftop penthouse added several new rooms, including a second kitchen

Stair section

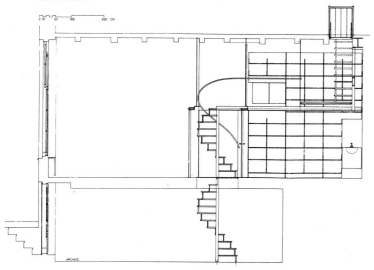

The project establishes new channels of vertical communication by mean of a metal spiral staircase, the directional nature of which is underlined by a light banister rail. The work was done in such a way that the installation of new materials and the creation of new connections do not conceal the original structures of the historical building.

Francesco Delogu & Gaetano Lixi
Castello Catrani

Umbria, Italy

Restoration of the Castello di Petriolo in a valley not far from Cittá di Castello, in the Italian district of Umbria, has resulted in refurbished interiors, fully adapted to modern living requirements, combined with total respect for the historical fabric of the building itself.

Built in medieval times as part of he nearby town's defensive network, the castle complex has numerous architectural stratifications testifying to the variety of uses it has been put to over the centuries, from noble residence to farming state house.

In 1736, Marco Antonio Catrani, counselor of th Roman Curia, redesigned the main façade, making two large bulwarks to access to courtyard, and some interior modifications.

The recent project by Delogu and Lixi focuses the conversion of the complex into a set of private dwellings. So they made a general conservative restoration plan and organized its division into four separate apartments.

The so-called chapel apartment featured here occupies only part of the wing to the left of the main portal. Its three-level design incorporates the previous layout without overwhelming it, creating beautifully contrived contrasts between austerity and complexity.

Photographs: Roberto Bossaglia

On this double page, several views of the iron walkway. It leads through the opening made in the thick supporting wall that separates it from the chapel and into the kitchen.

Julia B. Bolles & Peter L. Wilson
Dub House

Münster, Germany

This small addition to a 1960's Modernist atrium house respects the language of the object in which is found.

The team of architects Julia Bolles and Peter Wilson have made a careful and exquisite rehabilitation, based, as they declare, in the "fascination for clarity, optimism and simple geometries of the last days of functionalism".

The structure of the original house is transcended through the insertion of a new vertical element, a volume covered by intense blue brick that looks to the internal court. This foreign object, that emphasises and puts energy into the geometry of the complex, breaks through the artificial horizon of the existing flat roof.

Necessitated by new use requirements (a larger living space, a small studio) the new additions are reduced to five discrete elements: the blue glazed brick wall, the zinc wall, the sun louvers (a new horizontal factor), the internal swing wall and, as a nexus for the whole composition, the central fireplace.

Photographs: Christian Richters

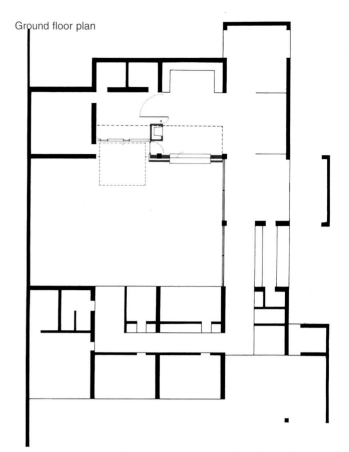

Ground floor plan

New intervention

Cross-section

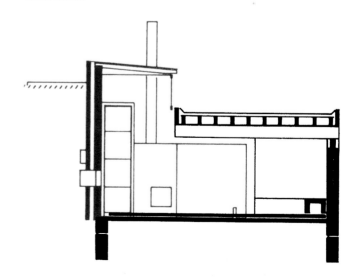

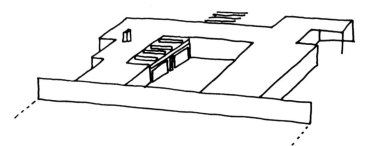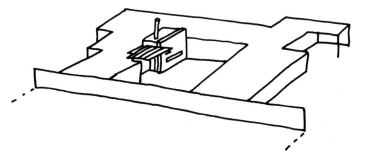

Sketches before and after the intervention

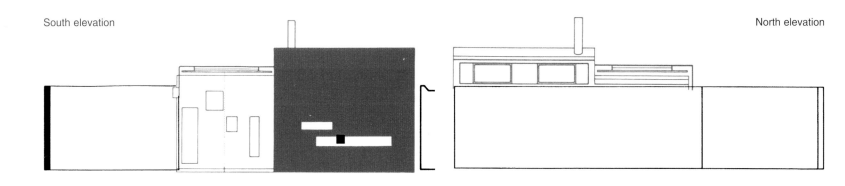

The project aims to solve the problems of space of the existing building by providing sufficient floor area to extend the living-room and create a small studio.

Cross-section

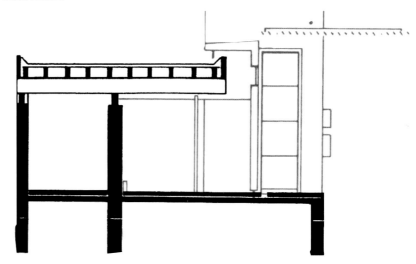

Rataplan
Bürombau Vienna Paint

Wien, Austria

An industrial workshop dating from 1899 was converted to provide the offices of a digital company. The commission was to contain workstations, computer room, scanner room, film processing equipment, etc. all cross-linked. Each of these fields also had to correspond to different requirements of acoustics, lighting and climate.

It was a very important starting point of the architectural concept to create no cells but to conserve the originally open space and generate views.

On the first floor there are offices, an exhibition space on the ground floor and a coffee house in an annexed. The entrance area is marked by a horizontal style plate, which to the depth of the space. A new staircase carries to the upper level where the offices are located. This staircase s formulated as an upright element linking the two floors. The existing lift was partly exposed by removing have been enlarged and transformed; now they give views of the industrial chimney and allow it to function inside the space.

In the upper floor the horizontal composition remains, by means of three freestanding, articulated shelf elements. As everything new in the building, these elements are se at an angle of 11º to the existing walls from the backbone of the space and accentuate the perspective. All abutments to existing walls and the roof are in glass to maintain the sense of spatial continuity.

On account of the different requirements, it had to be possible to close off the individual areas. Between the closed areas are the "work bays" of the zones without special acoustic and climatic requirements. The office in the middle of the space represents the 'market place' where clients are received.

Photographs: Markus Tomaselli

Three self-pporting shelving units placed at an angle of 11° against the walls of the building articulate the space and accentuate the effect of perspective. The elements of glass and perforated metal plate appear transparent and opaque according to the lighting.

Arnaud Goujon Architecte DPLG
Transformed penthouse

Paris, France

In the heart of Paris, the architect Arnaud Goujon transformed an old greenhouse located at the top of a block of flats into a small and comfortable refuge with a terrace and unique views. Conceived as an extension of the loft apartment, this volume would soon become the favorite room of this home.

It is a scheme in which the initial volume was respected and a new wooden frame was superimposed on the steel structure. On the exterior, the shingle boards are made of red Canadian cedar, while the interior walls are lined with moabi panels.

The main task for the architect in this rehabilitation – apart from the technical problems – consisted of designing and organizing the different spaces of the apartment, and resolving the problems of execution and assembly of the different materials.

The absence of exposed fittings on the wall panels of the interior helps to enlarge and unify the volume of the main room, which opens on both sides onto a terrace of 50 m2 covered with a jatoba wood deck and offering spectacular views of the urban landscape.

The interior of this unusual dwelling is composed only of a living room with an open integrated kitchen, in which a chimney is framed between two shelves, and a small bedroom with its bathroom. This room enjoys the benefit of two sources of natural light that illuminate this more private area: a small window in the back wall and a skylight located over the bed. The floor of the interior is made of chestnut parquet covered with white polyurethane paint that reduces the color saturation and brings freshness to the dwelling.

The wood, chosen for its plastic and structural qualities, is used as a double skin: soft and beautiful in the interior and rough and sturdy on the exterior. Thus, although this organic material is set against the urban nature of an environment in which steel is the main component, its form fits well into the geometric pattern of the building.

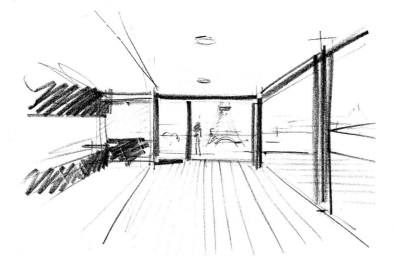

Photographs: Joel Cariou

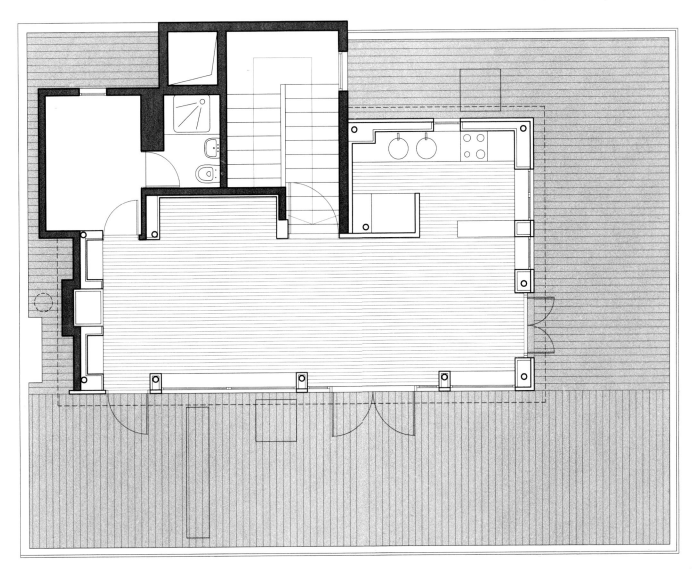

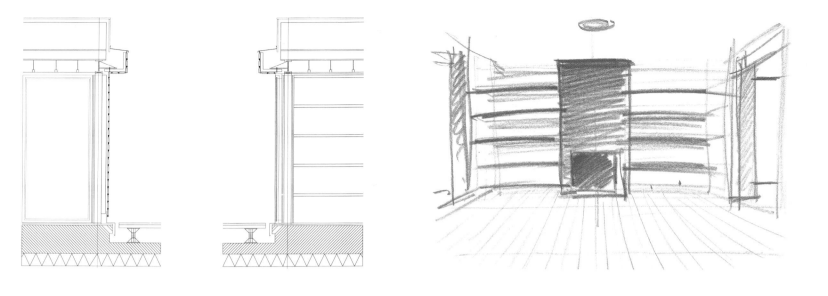